For Mum.

'This is my lanyard, Mum…'

PREFACE

This little book asks a big question:

> *What if we explored what is*
> *possible when leaders around*
> *the world bring the energy of*
> *love into every corner of their*
> *organization or institution?*
> *And when we also follow our*
> *leaders in doing that in our own*
> *lives?*

The text of this book is a letter I sent to The President of the United States in February 2014.

We have a new President now, and we always will; but the point was never what a President does, but what we do. Who are *we* being?

I believe answering the questions in this book could change everything.

Thank you for reading this.

David Firth

Loveland, Colorado
January 2017

The President of The United States of America
The White House
1600 Pennsylvania Avenue NW
Washington, DC 20500

February 14, 2014

Dear Mr President,

Is your work love made visible?

By way of introduction, my name is David Firth.
My work as a management consultant brings me
into contact with many businesses, firms and
institutions - both in the US and around the world
– and with the many thousands of ordinary
human beings who are employed in those places.
Every day my clients are looking for new ways to
be more effective and successful and, indeed,
happier.

Yet after twenty-three years of consulting, I find that there is one thing that has a huge impact on people's happiness, and that, despite all the advances we have made in our society, our relationship to this one thing has never shifted. I believe this thing to be one of the core reasons for individual suffering, social breakdown, and human conflict in our communities.

What is it? It is our unresolved relationship to work itself.

What I am writing to you about - and what I am now devoting my life to - is a movement whose existence is to repurpose and to re-hearten the place of work in our lives.

I want to uncover – for myself, for my family, for my community, for any country - what is possible when people live the truth of the famous line from Kahlil Gibran's *The Prophet*:

Work is love made visible.

I have built the foundation of this movement into my life and in my own work - and I am especially aware of this calling as two of my three sons are only a couple of years away from leaving education and entering 'the world of work.'

But I believe that the sort of mind shift that I am talking about here can have profound effects not just in terms of personal happiness and satisfaction, not just in terms of business effectiveness, but also how we govern and care for each other in society.

And so this letter is about a solution to the wider and recurrent issues in our global society:

> the breakdown of trust in almost everything and everybody, but especially in our institutions and organized religions;
>
> the fragmentation of society, and the organizations within them, into blocks, silos, us and them;

the loud demand for 'integrity' and 'accountability' in others, in parallel with an almost instinctual behavior of blame and finger-pointing;

the heaping of expectation upon - and our consequent and vocal disappointment with - 'new and better' leaders;

high incidences of stress and ill health of both body and mind accompanied by rising dependencies on alcohol and drugs for escape from those stressors;

ever-new strategies sought, and broadcast in every media outlet, for balancing two apparently separate things – work and life – when in fact there's only ever one thing to experience i.e. *being alive.*

I am sending copies of this letter to leaders in multiple facets of human endeavor – government, science, arts, charity and religion. I hold my message to be relevant to each and every one.

Work as Suffering- *The Status Quo*

It is so easy in our society to only think of work as a necessarily evil, the thing we have to do to pay the bills. Then we find that upwards of 40% of our life is consumed by our experience of work (and another 30% we are asleep!). And of course unhealthy experiences of work seep into the other aspects of our lives. There is no separation between those stressful feelings and family time, social time, community engagement and personal wellbeing. Sit with a friend unhappy in their work and notice what state they are in come Sunday evening.

It's not that many good people haven't been aware of this problem. I have been part of an industry –

academics, authors, coaches, consultants, practitioners etc. - that, over the last 30 years or so, have developed and disseminated many progressive ideas about work and institutional life. There has been a gradual shift – at the surface level at least – away from mechanistic, command & control assumptions about management and organization. And a shift toward a more enlightened concern with transformational leadership, employee engagement and the belief that 'people are our most important asset'- but yet not much has changed.

Beyond the theory – and the billions of dollars companies pour into the management consulting industry– statistics stubbornly resist this apparently enlightened progress. Aon Hewitt's 2013 *Consumer Health Mindset* report surveyed more than 2,800 employees and their dependents and found that almost half said their stress level was high or overwhelming. When asked the reasons for their stress, four out of five were work-related[1].

---

[1] *And the fifth was 'money worries'*
http://aon.mediaroom.com

Gallup's *State of the American Workplace: 2010-2012* report tells us that by the end of 2012, only 30% of American workers were engaged, or involved in, enthusiastic about, and committed to their workplace.

Even if this letter were only about improving the situation for business, a good question to ask would be this:

How healthy would our global economy be if the work satisfaction scores were nearer 100%?

The background conversation in our society is that you are special or lucky to love your work; and that suffering in it is the natural lot. I don't think anyone is out there yet with a strong enough presence to teach a different way of thinking. The best we get is advice on how to survive in the shark tank.

How can individuals feel fully expressed in their lives if over half of their waking lives they feel so imprisoned and oppressed? And how does that experience of constraint and imposition impact directly or indirectly, quickly or gradually, on business performance and, by extension, the productivity of a nation?

How many adults go to work every day in the United States alone? Roughly 150 million. And if the statistics are true, it means 105 million people are unhappy for over half of every waking, working day.

What drain is that on the possibility and innovation of a nation – or of the world?

So what is needed? The next management fad? A new essay on leadership in Harvard Business Review?

No.

We need something transformational, and yet
something profoundly pure and simple. It exists
right now in your home, Mr President, and in my
home too. We just need to let it out.

Looking Beyond the Pointing Finger –
The Turnaround

I remember when one of my first mentors made
me laugh when paraphrasing the Buddha: 'When I
point to the moon, the wise man looks where I'm
pointing; *my dog stares at my hand.*'

I believe that, in this era of great instability of
economic and social fragmentation, it is time we
stopped being satisfied with staring at our
teachers' hands.

Almost every way of thinking about human or
societal growth and progression is modeled as a
movement upwards. I want to look more closely
at what is waiting for us where 'up' is.

I believe it is time we woke up and acknowledged what most of us know to be the true. Upwards-facing organizational models and psychological theories are pointing to exactly the same place that the mystics, the world religions, and the poets have been encouraging us to look for ages. That finger is really pointing to mankind's highest expression and to our deepest reality:

> *What will survive of us is love.*
> *Philip Larkin*

I want to bring love out of the realm of religion, out of spirituality and poetry. I want to put it to work – literally – in our everyday reality.

I don't think I have met a leader in business who has not told me that his or her greatest and most heartfelt passion is their spouse and/or their children.

What if we explore what is possible when leaders around the world bring the energy of love into every corner of their organization or institution? And when we follow our leaders in doing that also?

Love Made Visible in Work - *The Vision*

> *...what is it to work with love?*
> *It is to weave the cloth with threads drawn from*
> *your heart, even as if your beloved were to wear*
> *that cloth.*
> *It is to build a house with affection,*
> *even as if your beloved were to dwell in that*
> *house.*
> *It is to sow seeds with tenderness and reap the*
> *harvest with joy, even as if your beloved were to*
> *eat the fruit.*
> *It is to charge all things you fashion with a breath*
> *of your own spirit.*
>
> *Khalil Gibran* The Prophet

I believe we could change the world if we were taught that work is love made visible.

I think such a teaching would help us all to:

- realize that the greatest gift we can give to the world is to be ourselves at its highest expression

- find every opportunity to serve the world and make a difference in it, whatever our present sphere of influence

- control the impulse to project any personal insecurity onto bosses or other employers

- see the creation of meaningful purpose as the source of wealth rather than the reward for it

- make healthy connections with other committed and passionate people around shared purpose, rather than invest in and exaggerate differences and comparisons with those we don't agree with

- have no need to be disappointed in other people. To see potential rather than limitation in others; to ask 'what if?' rather than 'why bother?'

It *is* possible to transform our relationship with work, from complaint to contribution. Much as some people react against this possibility as idealistic or patronizing to 'those less fortunate in employment than ourselves', it is in fact a common reality. We have all met someone who will sweep a floor from love rather than from protest; we have all met the cheery car park attendant, and the miserable one; we all have had the apparently banal yet actually transformational experience of being served in a restaurant by someone who cares about us - compared with those servers who want to show us how disaffected and demeaned they feel (and we know where we leave the bigger gratuity).

These people are out there now and everyday: people who shift their attitude as surely as others refuse to shift theirs; people who choose to come from a different place in their work, and by doing so transform the experience of that work for themselves and for everyone impacted by it.

From this place we can also transform our perceptions of problems or challenges. This is the stance of the *Hero's Journey* of Joseph Campbell, where every challenge or setback is seen as the source of learning or character development, a necessary step on the path, not a curse.

Where you stumble, there your treasure lies
Joseph Campbell

In most organizations I consult to, issues and problems are still considered a platform for blame and scapegoating, or a sign that something has gone wrong. If leaders could see that they are never given a challenge that they and their people aren't able to overcome with the application of creativity and community, there'd be a lot less fear in those organizations.

So I am proposing three understandings, three levels of thinking, about work. On a personal level, this is what I want to teach my three sons:

1. Consciously and deliberately seek work that you love

2. Do any work that you are given with and from love

And then there's the third:

3. Be love - and work that.

This third level brings us to the essence of being human: who are we and how do we choose to live?

It asks us also to look at the essence of being an organization, since any organization is only ever an outward expression of its creators, its people. There is still much confusion about this. So many CEOs or business owners are apparently completely comfortable that the purpose of an

organization is to create profit for its shareholders
– and then will justify any subsequent un-integral
behavior from that place. But there has to be
more than this. As the British author and
philosopher Charles Handy reminds us, to say that
the primary reason a company exists is to create
profit for its shareholders is a little like saying the
primary reason a human being exists is to breathe
in and out.

The truth of the matter is that we all get to declare
what the purpose of anything is, including our
lives and our work. And we can either stare at the
hand or look to the moon.

When I realize that the etymology of the word
work in Old English is not *job* or *earn* or *labor* but a
verb meaning *to make, to create*, I begin to see that
my life is my work, my *life's work* is exactly that. It
is what I create every day. It's how I show up
every day.

It's how I impact other people – friends, family, associates, customers, every day. *That* is what is being made visible. What do I choose to make visible? I choose love.

Work as Love Made Visible – *How We Get There*

What we are facing in the world is a challenge of consciousness.

Love is in the same realm of consciousness as innovation and creativity and purpose and connection and service and joy (all the things commonly cited as *what's wanted* or *what's missing* when people complain about their work).

All of these qualities are expressions of higher human consciousness – whereas the fear and anger and the separation that plagues so many of our institutions are natural outcomes of lower levels of consciousness.

The challenge is for us all is to keep rising 'up', to keep re-connecting to higher levels of consciousness as a day-to-day practice. But *How?*

How *do* human beings raise their level of consciousness? How *do* we look for the moon rather than stare at the pointing hand?

It requires a radical shift in *how we are thinking*. And I don't know any other way to shift the mind consistently than to shift *what we talk about*. And I know that to shift what we talk about requires that we start the conversation with *a question we haven't asked before*. Here's mine:

I believe that work is love made visible. If that were true for you too, what would shift in your leadership and the lives of the people you lead?

I would love to hear your answer to this question, Mr President. Would you be willing to write back, share your answer and begin a dialogue?

And how can I help? How can I serve you – and the people around you - in making the answer to that question a reality?

Because that is my work.

Work as love made visible.

Thank you for reading this.

Yours sincerely,

David Firth

DAVID FIRTH

People draw together by their very nature,
but habit and custom keep them apart
Translated from Confucius

David is a consultant, facilitator, change management expert, conference speaker and executive coach in progressive Organizational Development. His latest two books are *From 'Making a Living' to Creating a Life* and the subject of his recent TEDx talk, *Change Your World One Word at a Time.*

He specializes in generating powerful conversations amongst his clients for greater business and personal results.

David helps global clients – and those nearer to his home in Colorado - institute profound practices for engagement, enrolment and workforce participation. He brings people back to being the source rather than the victims or objects of change.

David works with companies who want to build relationships with their stakeholders based on respect, commitment, accountability and mutuality.

Current clients include the International Olympic Committee, Amnesty International, Unilever and a globally-famous family confectionary business.

As a consultant he specializes in complex, intractable problems; areas where interventions have brought limited or temporary progress, and in 'difficult' relationships or personalities.

At the heart of all David's work is his proprietary BIGGER FUTURES PROCESS and CONVERSATIONS FOR CHANGE methodologies, which are guaranteed to generate creativity, energy and accountability where there was only resistance, stasis and blame in the past. David is expert in both small and (very) large group facilitation such as OPEN SPACE and WORLD CAFE, and his consulting practice also incorporates executive coaching and innovative personal development workshops.

David's website is www.davidfirth.com and he can be reached at david@davidfirth.com

www.ingramcontent.com/pod-product-compliance
Lightning Source LLC
Chambersburg PA
CBHW022058190326
41520CB00008B/808